Little Skill Seekers

CONNECT THE DOTS

■SCHOLASTIC

New York • Toronto • London • Auckland • Sydney • New Delhi
Mexico City • Hong Kong • Buenos Aires

Cover Design: Tannaz Fassihi
Cover Illustration: Michael Robertson
Interior Design: Mina Chen
Interior Illustration: Doug Jones

ISBN: 978-1-338-25560-7

1 2 3 4 5 6 7 8 9 10   40   24 23 22 21 20 19 18

Dear Parent,

Welcome to *Little Skill Seekers: Connect the Dots*! Hand-eye coordination and fine-motor skills are important early writing skills—this workbook will help your child develop these skills.

Help your little skill seeker build a strong foundation for learning by choosing more books in the Little Skill Seekers series. The exciting and colorful workbooks in the series are designed to set your child on the path to success. Each book targets essential skills important to your child's development.

Here are some key features of *Little Skill Seekers: Connect the Dots* and the other workbooks in this series:

- Filled with colorful illustrations that make learning fun and playful

- Provides plenty of opportunity to practice essential skills

- Builds independence as children work through the pages on their own, at their own pace

- Comes in a perfect size that fits easily in a backpack for practice on the go

Now let's get started on this journey to help your child become a successful, lifelong learner!

—The Editors

Connect the dots from 1 to 5. Then color the picture.

Connect the dots from 1 to 5. Then color the picture.

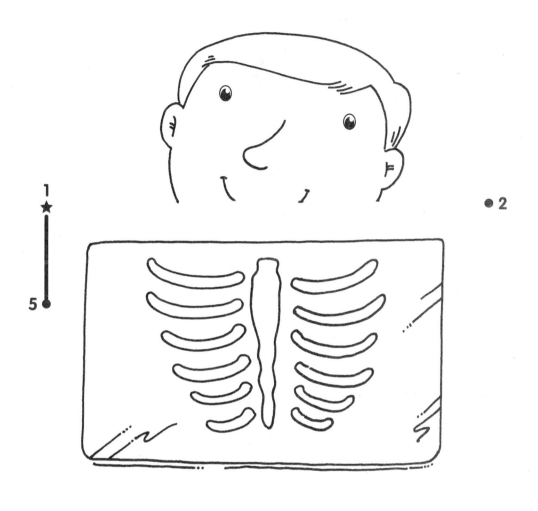

1
★

5 ●

● 2

● 4

● 3

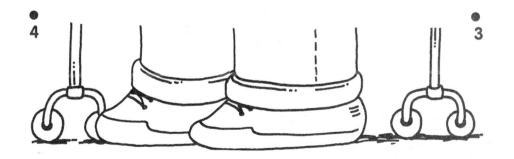

Connect the dots from 1 to 5. Then color the picture.

Connect the dots from 1 to 5. Then color the picture.

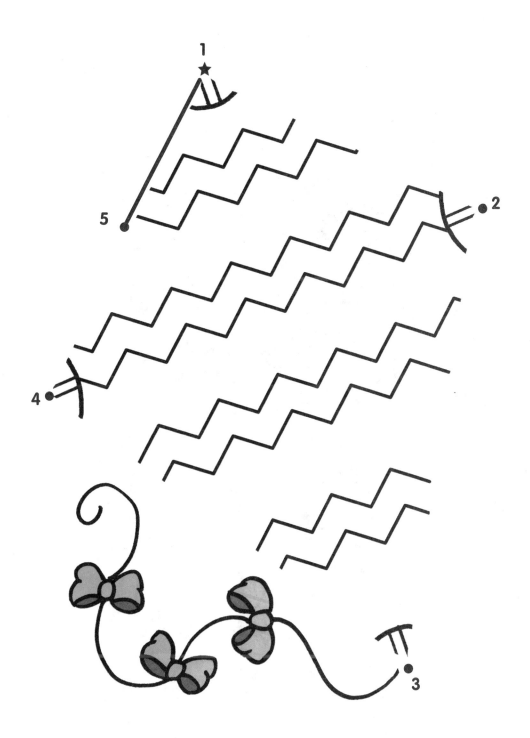

Connect the dots from 1 to 5. Then color the picture.

© Scholastic Inc.

Connect the dots from 1 to 6. Then color the picture.

Connect the dots from 1 to 6. Then color the picture.

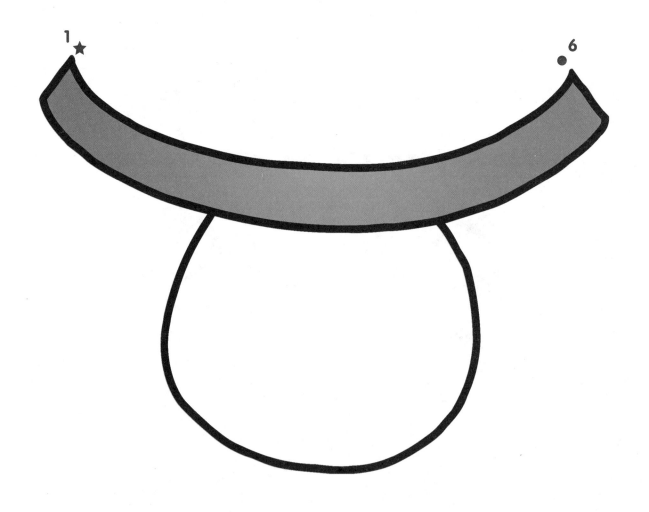

Connect the dots from 1 to 7. Then color the picture.

Connect the dots from 1 to 8. Then color the picture.

Connect the dots from 1 to 8. Then color the picture.

Connect the dots from 1 to 8. Then color the picture.

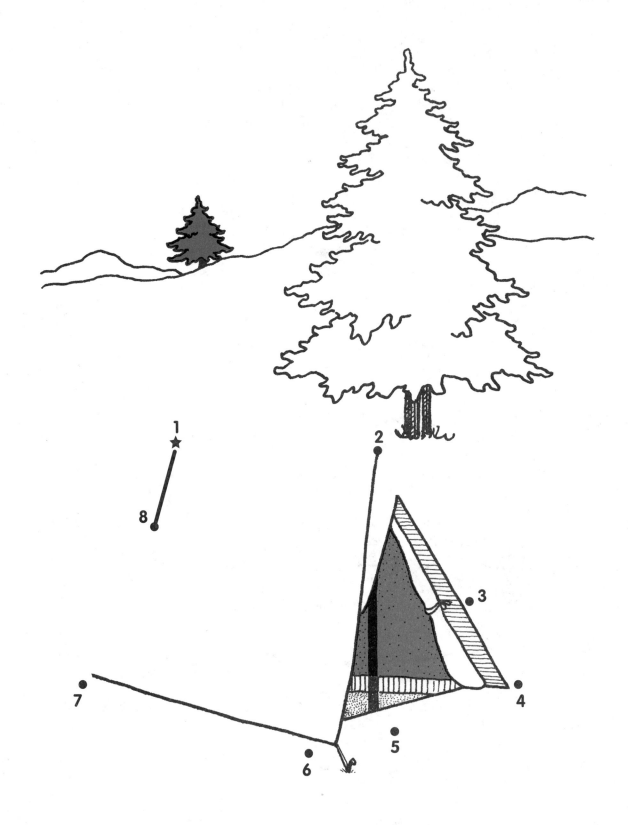

Connect the dots from 1 to 9. Then color the picture.

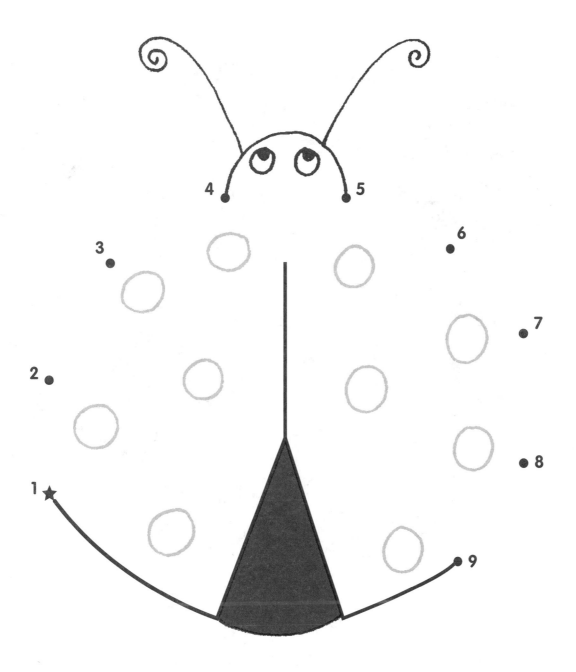

Connect the dots from 1 to 9. Then color the picture.

Connect the dots from 1 to 10. Then color the picture.

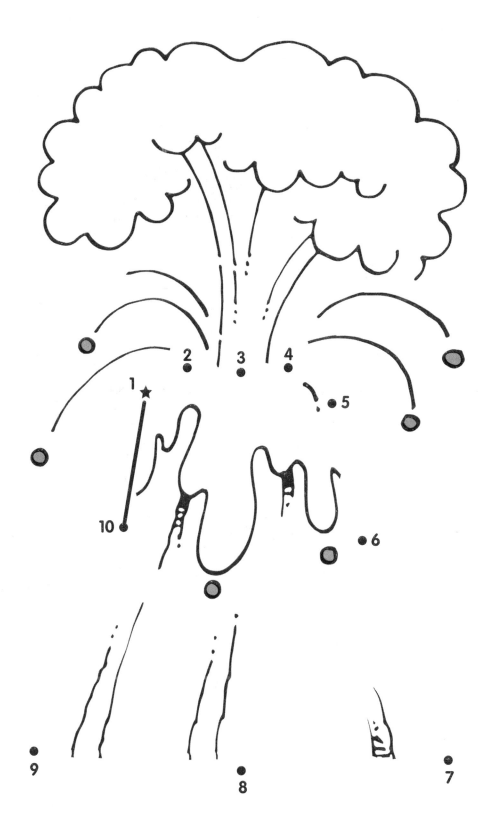

Connect the dots from 1 to 10. Then color the picture.

Connect the dots from 1 to 10. Then color the picture.

Connect the dots from 1 to 10. Then color the picture.

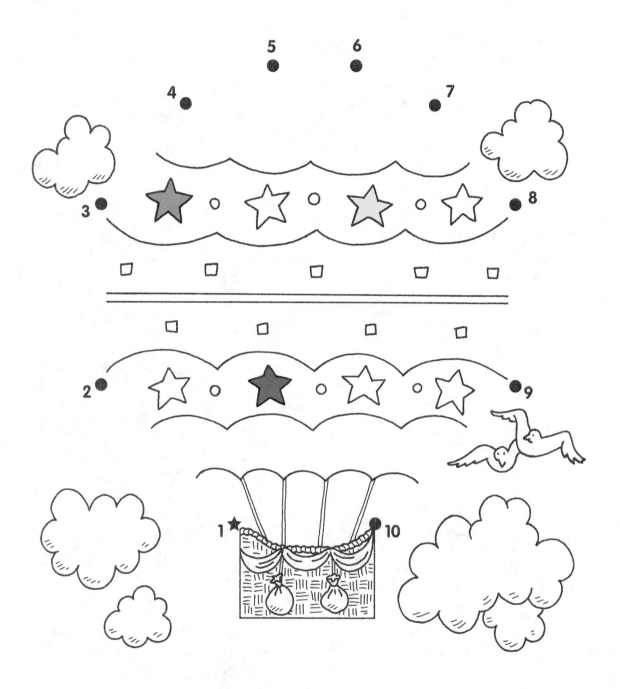

Connect the dots from 1 to 10. Then color the picture.

Connect the dots from 1 to 10. Then color the picture.

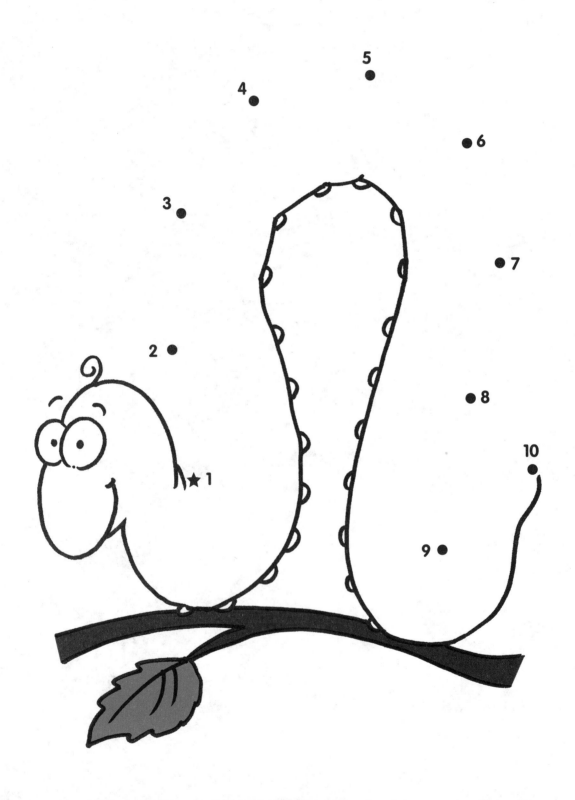

Connect the dots from 1 to 11. Then color the picture.

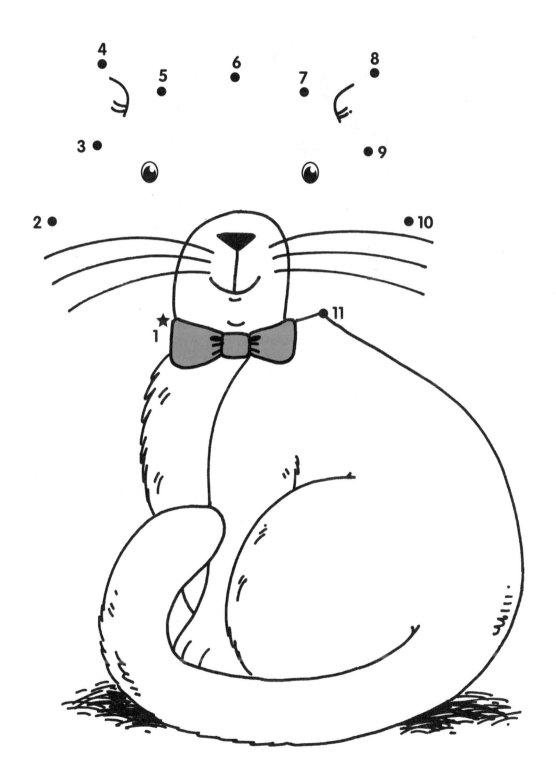

Connect the dots from 1 to 11. Then color the picture.

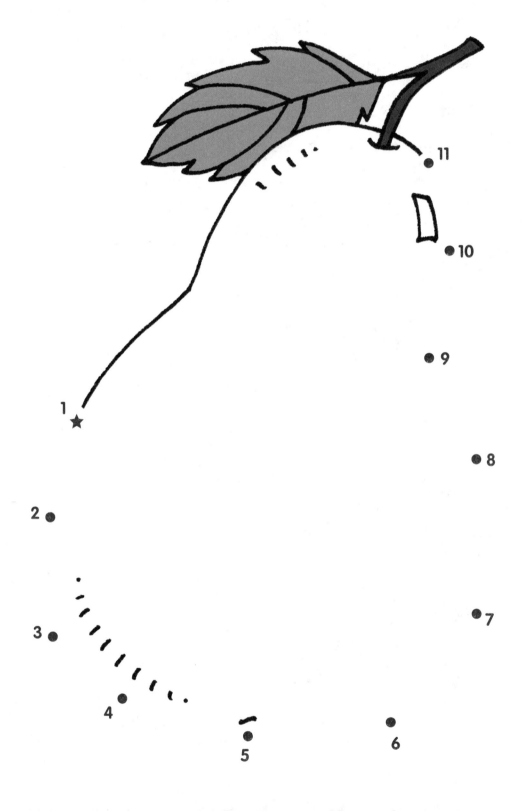

Connect the dots from 1 to 12. Then color the picture.

Connect the dots from 1 to 12. Then color the picture.

Connect the dots from 1 to 13. Then color the picture.

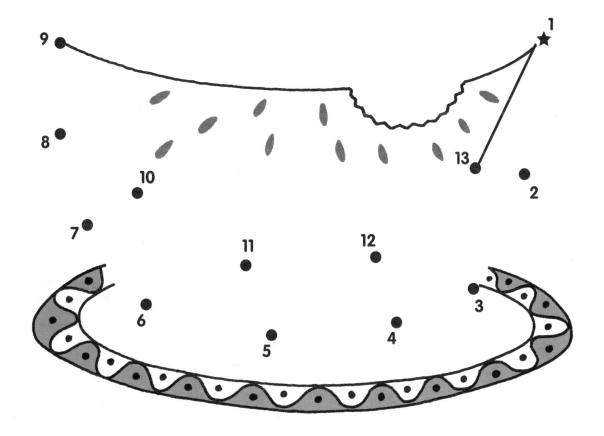

Connect the dots from 1 to 13. Then color the picture.

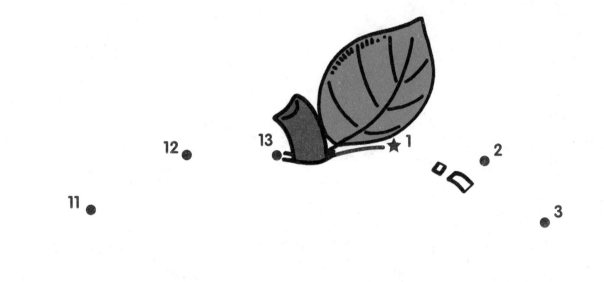

12

11

10

9

8

13

1

2

3

4

5

6

7

Connect the dots from 1 to 14. Then color the picture.

Connect the dots from 1 to 14. Then color the picture.

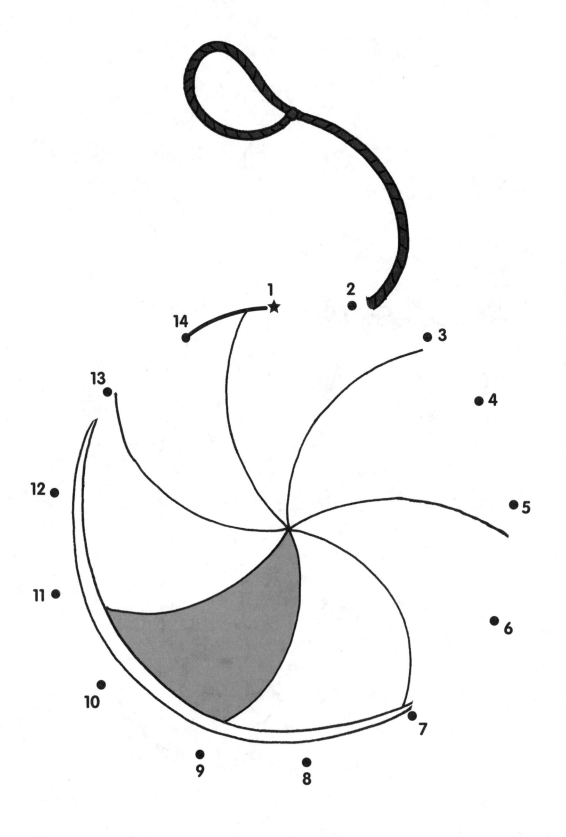

Connect the dots from 1 to 15. Then color the picture.

U.S.A.

Connect the dots from 1 to 15. Then color the picture.

7

6

5

8

9

4

10

11   3

1

2

12

13

14

15

Connect the dots from 1 to 15. Then color the picture.

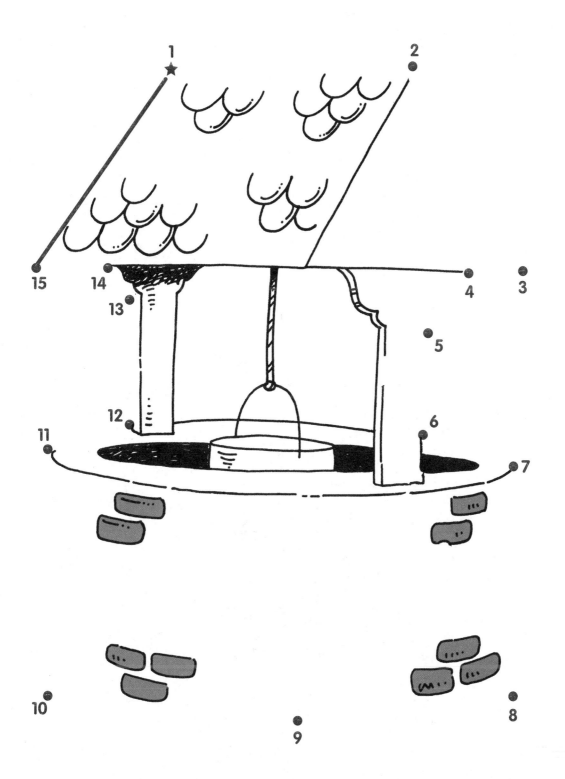

Connect the dots from 1 to 15. Then color the picture.

Connect the dots from 1 to 15. Then color the picture.

Connect the dots from 1 to 16. Then color the picture.

7

8

9

10

6

11

5

12

4

13

3

14

2

15

1 ★

16

Connect the dots from 1 to 16. Then color the picture.

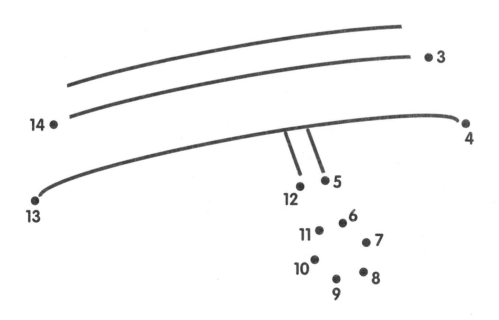

★1

16 •

• 2

15 •

• 3

14 •

• 4

13 •

12 •

• 5

• 6

11 •

• 7

10 •

• 8

9 •

Connect the dots from 1 to 17. Then color the picture.

Connect the dots from 1 to 17. Then color the picture.

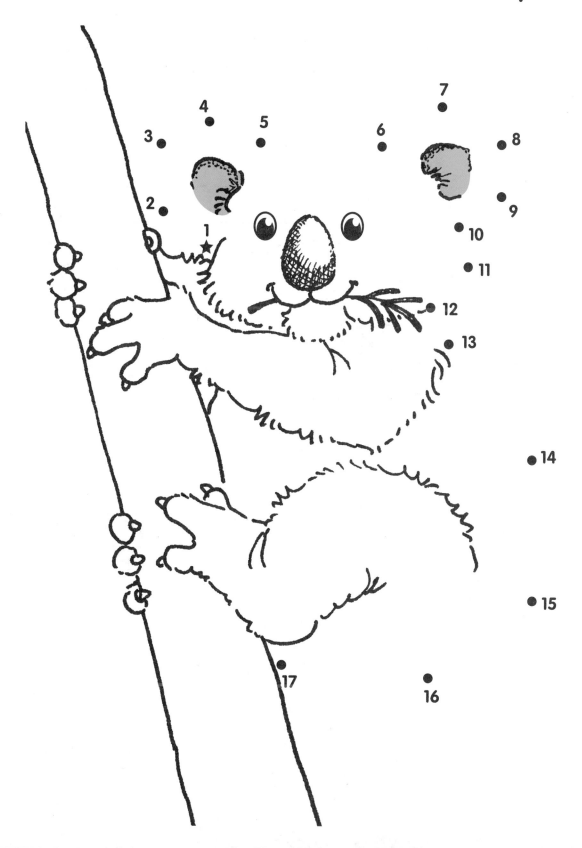

3
4
5
6
7
8
2
9
1
10
11
12
13
14
15
17
16

Connect the dots from 1 to 18. Then color the picture.

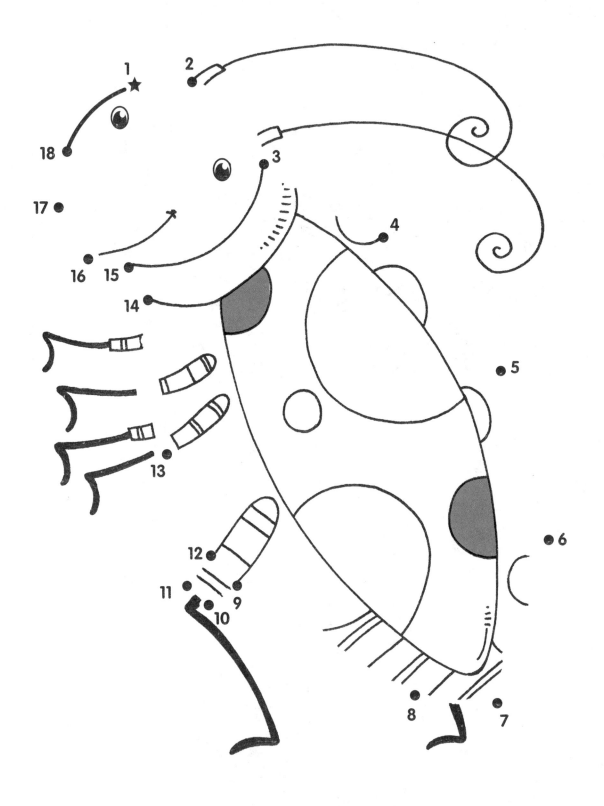

Connect the dots from 1 to 18. Then color the picture.

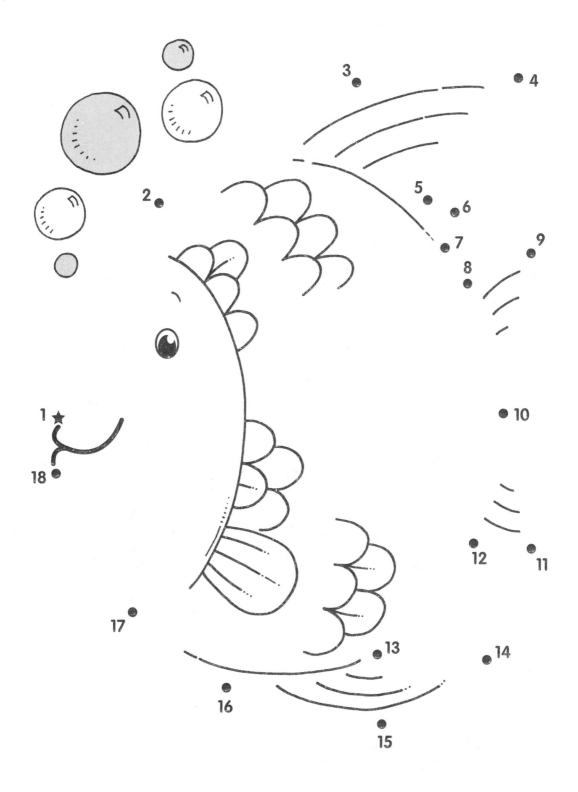

Connect the dots from 1 to 19. Then color the picture.

8

7

6

5

4

3

2

9

10

11

13

15

14

12

1

16

17

18

19

Connect the dots from 1 to 19. Then color the picture.

Connect the dots from 1 to 20. Then color the picture.

Connect the dots from 1 to 20. Then color the picture.

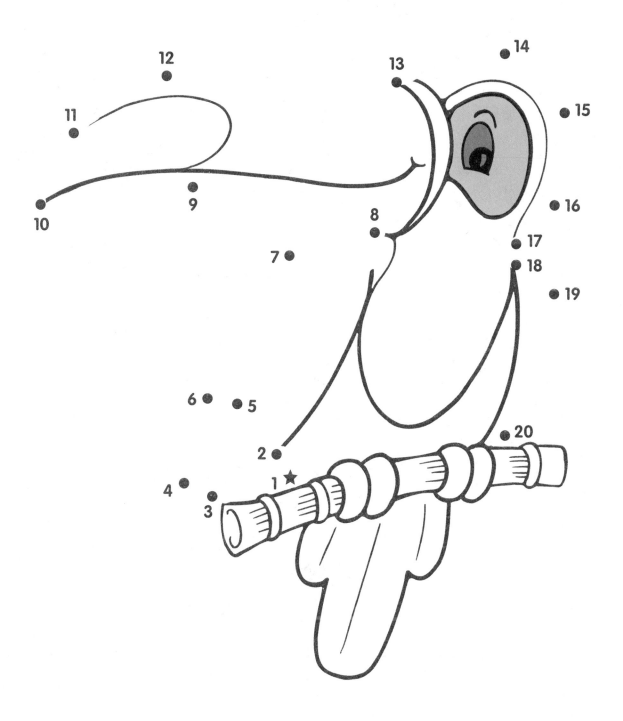

Connect the dots from 1 to 20. Then color the picture.

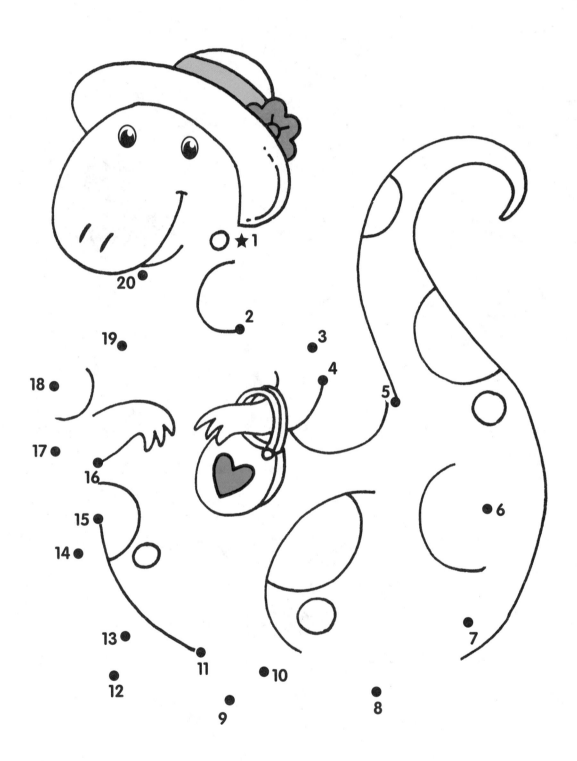

Connect the dots from 1 to 20. Then color the picture.

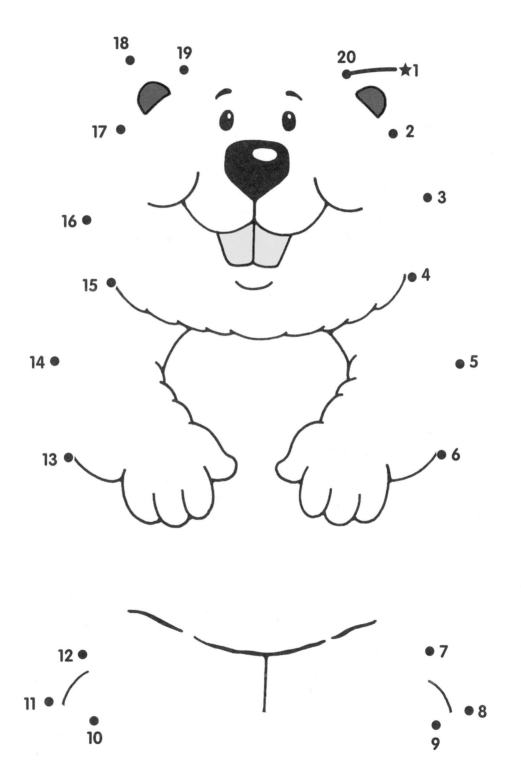

Connect the dots from 1 to 20. Then color the picture.

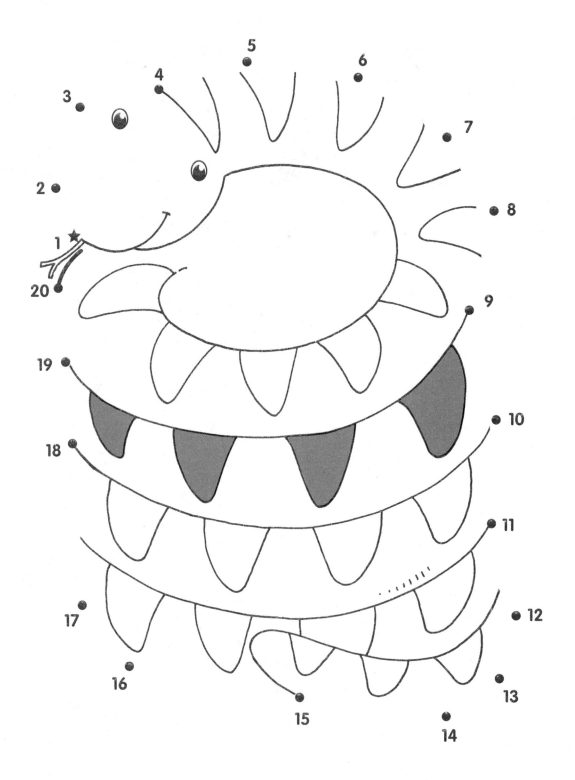